A Benjamin and his Inquis Guide

Northern Ireland

Anita Ganeri

raintree

a Capstone company — publishers for children

Raintree is an imprint of Capstone Global Library Limited, a company incorporated in England and Wales having its registered office at 264 Banbury Road, Oxford, OX2 7DY – Registered company number: 6695582

www.raintree.co.uk
myorders@raintree.co.uk

Edited by Helen Cox Cannons
Designed by Philippa Jenkins
Original illustrations © Capstone Global Library Limited 2016
Original map illustration by Oxford Designers and Illustrators
Ben and Barko illustrated by Sernur ISIK
Picture research by Tracy Cummins
Production by Victoria Fitzgerald
Originated by Capstone Global Library Limited
Printed and bound in China

ISBN 978 1 4747 1466 2
19 18 17 16 15
10 9 8 7 6 5 4 3 2 1

British Library Cataloguing in Publication Data
A full catalogue record for this book is available from the British Library.

Acknowledgements
We would like to thank the following for permission to reproduce photographs: Alamy: Ivan Vdovin, 18 Left, LiamMcArdle.com, 18 Right, Nature Picture Library/Robert Thompson, 27, Paul Lindsay, 8, scenicireland.com/Christopher Hill Photographic, 10, 17, Simon Reddy, 20, Stuwdamdorp, 15; Corbis: Destinations, 23, 29; Getty Images: AFP PHOTO/JEWEL SAMAD, 16, AFP PHOTO/Peter Muhly, 19, Chris Hill, 6, David Cannon, 22, VisitBritain/Britain on View, 14, Wilhelmina van Rijn e/v Andeweg, 24; iStockphoto: bogdanhoria, Cover, Peter Zelei, 11; National Geographic Creative: CHRIS HILL, 25; Shutterstock: Brent Hofacker, 21, Pierre Leclerc, 9, Rainer Lesniewski, 5, Serg Zastavkin, 4, Thitipat Vatanasirithum, 28; SuperStock: Design Pics, 13, The Irish Image Collection, 12; Thinkstock: Jen Grantham, 26, RogerBradley, 7

Every effort has been made to contact copyright holders of material reproduced in this book. Any omissions will be rectified in subsequent printings if notice is given to the publisher.

All the internet addresses (URLs) given in this book were valid at the time of going to press. However, due to the dynamic nature of the internet, some addresses may have changed, or sites may have changed or ceased to exist since publication. While the author and publisher regret any inconvenience this may cause readers, no responsibility for any such changes can be accepted by either the author or the publisher.

Some words are shown in bold, **like this**. You can find out what they mean by looking in the glossary.

Contents

Welcome to Northern Ireland!

Hello! My name's Benjamin Blog and this is Barko Polo, my **inquisitive** dog. (He's named after ancient ace explorer **Marco Polo**.) We have just got back from our latest adventure – exploring Northern Ireland. We put this book together from some of the blog posts we wrote on the way.

ATLANTIC OCEAN

North Channel

NORTHERN
IRELAND

ANTRIM

DERRY/LONDONDERRY

TYRONE

Loch
Neagh

BELFAST

FERMANAGH

ARMAGH

DOWN

Irish Sea

REPUBLIC OF IRELAND (EIRE)

BARKO'S BLOG-TASTIC NORTHERN IRELAND FACTS

Northern Ireland is a small country in the north-east corner of the island of Ireland. It is part of the United Kingdom. The rest of the island is called the Republic of Ireland.

Stories of Northern Ireland

Posted by: Ben Blog | 30 July at 3.01 p.m.

We're starting our tour in County Tyrone. Barko and I wanted to see the famous Beaghmore stone circles. They date back to around 4,000 years ago, during the early **Bronze Age**. The seven circles might have been used as meeting places or for religious ceremonies. No one really knows.

BARKO'S BLOG-TASTIC NORTHERN IRELAND FACTS

These are the Parliament Buildings in Belfast. They are named Stormont. The government of Northern Ireland meets there. Northern Ireland is part of the United Kingdom but it makes its own laws.

Geography and giants

Today Barko and I set off early to explore **Lough** Neagh. Lough Neagh is the largest lake in the British Isles. Legend says that it was formed by a giant called Finn McCool. He scooped up a lump of earth to throw at a rival giant across the sea in Scotland. The dip left behind filled with water to form the lough.

BARKO'S BLOG-TASTIC NORTHERN IRELAND FACTS

Giant's Causeway in County Antrim is made of thousands of **hexagonal** blocks of rock. The rock was thrown up by ancient volcanic eruptions. Finn McCool is said to have built it so that he could cross the sea.

Mountains and glens

We have come to the Mourne Mountains in County Down. I wanted to climb Slieve Donard, which is the highest peak in Northern Ireland. It stands at 850 metres (2,789 feet) tall. It's quite an easy climb to the top along the new stone path. The views are amazing!

BARKO'S BLOG-TASTIC NORTHERN IRELAND FACTS

The nine Glens of Antrim are one of Northern Ireland's top beauty spots. They are valleys carved out by Ice Age **glaciers**. This is Glenariff, the biggest glen.

City sight-seeing

We've arrived in Belfast, the capital city of Northern Ireland. Belfast lies at the mouth of the River Lagan, where it flows into Belfast **Lough**. Belfast's location made it an important **port** and centre for shipbuilding. We're going to catch a tourist bus to visit some of the city's top sights.

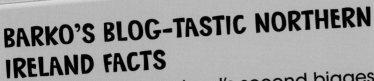

BARKO'S BLOG-TASTIC NORTHERN IRELAND FACTS

Derry is Northern Ireland's second biggest city after Belfast. The old city of Derry is surrounded by 400-year-old walls. You can walk all the way around the wall to get a bird's-eye view of the town.

Hoo's things?

Posted by: Ben Blog | 1 November at 7.59 p.m.

About 1.8 million people live in Northern Ireland. Most people speak English. Some people also speak Irish and Ulster Scots. *Hoo's things?* means "How are you?" in Ulster Scots. You could answer *Not that guid* ("Not very well") or *Brave an guid* ("Very well").

→

✈ **N1**

Béal Feirste

BELFAST

Aerphort

BARKO'S BLOG-TASTIC NORTHERN IRELAND FACTS

Irish and Ulster Scots are an important part of Northern Irish culture. Some signs, like this one, appear in two languages – Irish and English.

Schools and homes

Posted by: Ben Blog | 5 January at 9.15 a.m.

Northern Irish children start school when they are four or five years old. Most schools teach pupils in English but some schools teach some subjects in Irish. Schools have long summer holidays (July and August) but they have shorter holidays during the rest of the year.

BARKO'S BLOG-TASTIC NORTHERN IRELAND FACTS

Many people in Northern Ireland live in modern houses and flats. There are also traditional houses, such as these on Rathlin Island. There are around 100 people living on the island.

Beliefs and celebrations

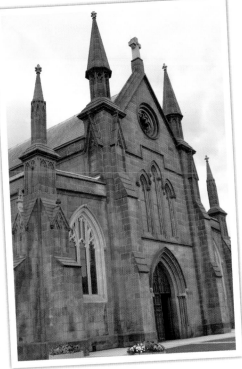

Most people in Northern Ireland are **Christians**. They belong to the **Roman Catholic** Church or the **Protestant** Church. In Armagh there are two beautiful **cathedrals**. One is Roman Catholic (left); the other is Protestant (right). They are both named St Patrick, after the **patron saint** of Ireland.

BARKO'S BLOG-TASTIC NORTHERN IRELAND FACTS

On 17 March, people in Northern Ireland celebrate St Patrick's Day. There are colourful street parades, like this one. This is in Downpatrick, where St Patrick is said to be buried.

Hearty breakfast

Next morning, Barko and I decided to treat ourselves to a traditional Northern Irish breakfast. It is called an Ulster Fry. You get bacon, sausages, eggs, tomato, mushrooms and fried soda bread. I think we're going to need a very long walk now!

BARKO'S BLOG-TASTIC NORTHERN IRELAND FACTS

Potatoes are a key ingredient in Northern Irish food. Popular potato dishes include champ (mashed potato with spring onions), boxty (potato cake) and potato farl (potato bread).

boxty

Having fun

We are in Portrush, a town on the north coast, watching some golf. Some of the world's top golfers come from Northern Ireland, such as Rory McIlroy (below). But sssh, we've got to be quiet! The next golfer's about to start to play. This is called **teeing off**.

BARKO'S BLOG-TASTIC NORTHERN IRELAND FACTS

This dancer is performing a traditional Irish stepdance. She holds her upper body still while she performs some very quick, fancy footwork. There are group and **solo** Irish stepdances.

From shipwrecks to shipbuilding

Posted by: Ben Blog | 23 May at 2.31 p.m.

We're visiting Titanic Belfast. This is a huge exhibition about the famous ship the *Titanic*. The *Titanic* was launched in Belfast in 1911. It then sank on its way to the United States. The exhibition has lots of objects, such as letters, notebooks and menus, from the ship.

BARKO'S BLOG-TASTIC NORTHERN IRELAND FACTS

These two gigantic cranes are nicknamed Samson and Goliath. They can lift over 800 tonnes each! They are owned by a company called Harland and Wolff. The company used to be one of the largest shipbuilders in the world.

And finally...

It's our last day. Barko and I have come to Carrickfergus. We want to explore its castle, which was built in 1177 on the shore of Belfast **Lough**. The castle stood guard over the town of Carrickfergus for hundreds of years. In World War II, it was used as an **air-raid shelter.**

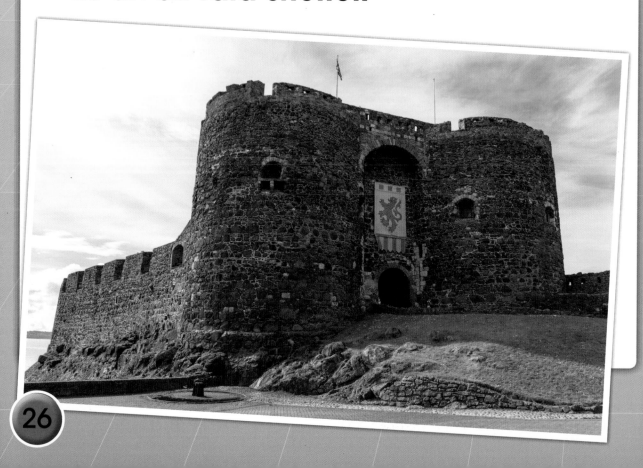

BARKO'S BLOG-TASTIC NORTHERN IRELAND FACTS

These Marble Arch Caves in County Fermanagh were carved out by an underground river. This river flowed off the mountains and created these caves. The caves are 11.5 kilometres (7.1 miles) long. Lucky we had a torch with us!

Northern Ireland fact file

Area: 14,135 square kilometres (5,457 square miles)

Population: 1,841,245 (2014)

Capital city: Belfast

Other main cities: Derry, Lisburn, Newtownabbey

Languages: English, Irish, Ulster Scots

Main religions: Christianity

Highest mountain: Slieve Donard
(850 metres/2,789 feet)

Longest river: Bann (129 kilometres/80 miles)

Currency: Pound sterling

Northern Ireland quiz

Find out how much you know about Northern Ireland with our quick quiz.

1. Which city was the famous ship *Titanic* launched from?
a) Derry
b) Belfast
c) Lisburn

2. How many Glens of Antrim are there?
a) 7
b) 2
c) 9

3. Which is the highest mountain in Northern Ireland?
a) Slieve Donard
b) Snowdon
c) Carrauntoohil

4. What is potato farl?
a) potato crisps
b) baked potato
c) potato bread

5. What is this?

Answers
1. b
2. c
3. a
4. c
5. Irish stepdancing

29

Glossary

air-raid shelter underground or sheltered hiding place; during wartime, it would keep people safe during a bomb or rocket attack by aircraft

Bronze Age period of time between c. 2500 BC and 300 BC; the Bronze Age came just after the Stone Age and before the Iron Age

cathedral large, important church

glacier huge river of ice

hexagonal having six sides

inquisitive interested in learning about the world

lough Irish word for lake or bay

Marco Polo explorer who lived from about 1254 to 1324; he travelled from Italy to China

patron saint saint who is special to a particular country or place

port place by the sea or a river for loading and unloading ships

Protestant type of Christianity that separated from the Roman Catholic religion during the 16th century

Roman Catholic type of Christian religion that has the pope as its head

solo on your own

teeing off when a golfer hits the first shot to start to play his or her game

Find out more

Books

Countries in Our World: United Kingdom, Michael Burgan (Franklin Watts, 2013)

Discover Countries: United Kingdom, Tim Atkinson (Wayland, 2013)

Ireland (Countries Around the World), Melanie Waldron (Raintree, 2012)

Websites

ngkids.co.uk/places

National Geographic's website has lots of information, photos and maps of countries around the world.

www.worldatlas.com

Packed with information about different countries, this website has flags, time zones, facts and figures, maps and timelines.

Index